# In These Walls and Floors

Nancy Harris

Raintree

Chicago, Illinois

**www.heinemannraintree.com**
Visit our website to find out more information about Heinemann-Raintree books.

**To order:**
☎ Phone 888-454-2279
🖳 Visit www.heinemannraintree.com to browse our catalog and order online.

2010 Raintree
an imprint of Capstone Global Library, LLC
Chicago, Illinois

Edited by Rebecca Rissman, Nancy Dickmann, and Sian Smith
Designed by Joanna Hinton-Malivoire
Original illustrations © Capstone Global Library LLC, 2010
Illustrated by Kevin Rechin
Picture research by Tracy Cummins and Heather Mauldin
Originated by Capstone Global Library Ltd
Printed and bound in China by Leo Paper Products Ltd

14 13 12 11 10
10 9 8 7 6 5 4 3 2 1

**Library of Congress Cataloging-in-Publication Data**
Harris, Nancy, 1956-
  In these walls and floors / Nancy Harris.
    p. cm. -- (What's lurking in this house?)
  Includes bibliographical references and index.
  ISBN 978-1-4109-3727-8 (
  ISBN 978-1-4109-3733-9 (pb)
1. Household pests--Juvenile literature. 2. Interior walls--Juvenile literature. 3. Floors--Juvenile literature. 4. House cleaning--Juvenile literature. I. Title.
  TX325.H272 2010
  648'.5--dc22

                    2009022162

**Acknowledgments**
The author and publisher are grateful to the following for permission to reproduce copyright material: Alamy pp.**7**, **22** (© blickwinkel); Ardea p.**23** (© Johan de Meester); Bugwood.org pp.**13** (© Scott Bauer, USDA Agricultural Research Service), **16** (© Joseph Berger); Dwight Kuhn Photography p.**11** (© Dwight Kuhn); FLPA p.**21** (© Nigel Cattlin); Getty Images p.**15** (AFP/Torsten Silz); Minden p.**9** (© Christian Ziegler); Nature Picture Library p.**17** (© Dietmar Nill), **18** (© Kim Taylor); Shutterstock pp.**25** (© Alexander Dvorak), **26** (© Postnikova Kristina), **28** (© Semen Lixodeev), **29 bat** (© javarman), **29 rat** (© Pakhnyushcha), **29 termite** (© Dr. Morley Read).

Cover photograph of a brown rat reproduced with permission of FLPA (© Derek Middleton).

Some words are shown in bold, **like this**. You can find out what they mean by looking in the glossary.

# Contents

# Is Something Lurking in This House?

A house is a place where you eat, sleep, work, and play. You know every wall and floor in your house. But do you know about everything that is living in your house?

# Creak, Moan

The walls and floors in your house creak and moan. This can happen when the wind blows or you step on a loose floorboard.

rat

But the noises you hear could also be
caused by creatures in your home.

# Terrible Termites

Termites are insects that love to eat wood. They like to live in large groups called **colonies**. There can be thousands of termites in a colony.

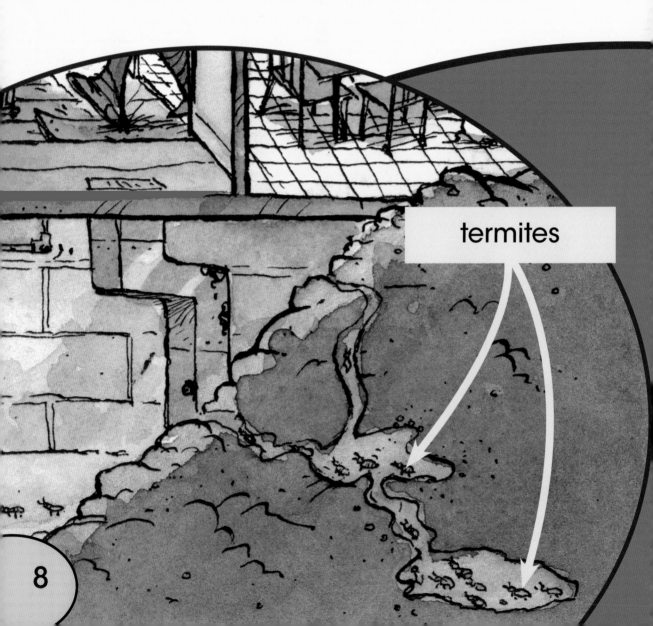

termites

## FUN FACT

Subterranean termites don't live in your house. They just like eating it. Every night they return to the soil outside where they live.

# Hard Workers

Each termite in the **colony** has a job. The **worker termites** in the group go out and get food for the others. They may go into houses to get food.

## FUN FACT

Worker termites do not sleep. They work 24 hours a day!

You can spot a worker termite by its white color.

# Wood Eaters

**Worker termites** need to eat a lot of wood to feed the rest of the **colony**. They may eat:

- window sills
- floorboards
- porch steps
- beams

Sometimes termites eat wallpaper too.

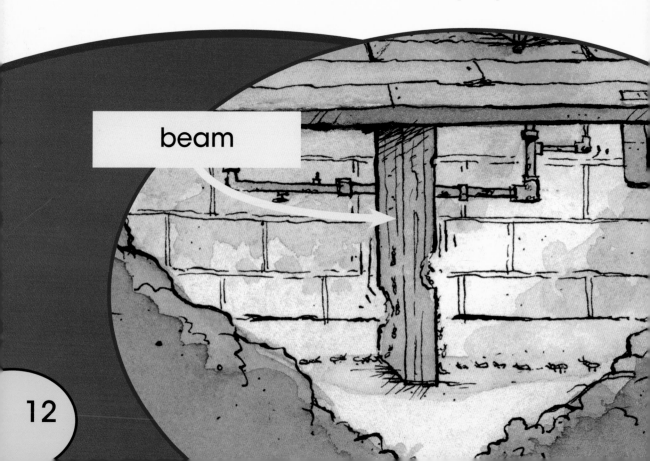

beam

Termites can cause a lot of damage to the wood in people's homes.

13

# Bats in the Attic

Bats are **mammals**. They have wings and fur. Some bats like to live in houses. The place where they sleep is called a **roost**. Look around. You may find bats in your **attic**. You may find bats on the roof of your house.

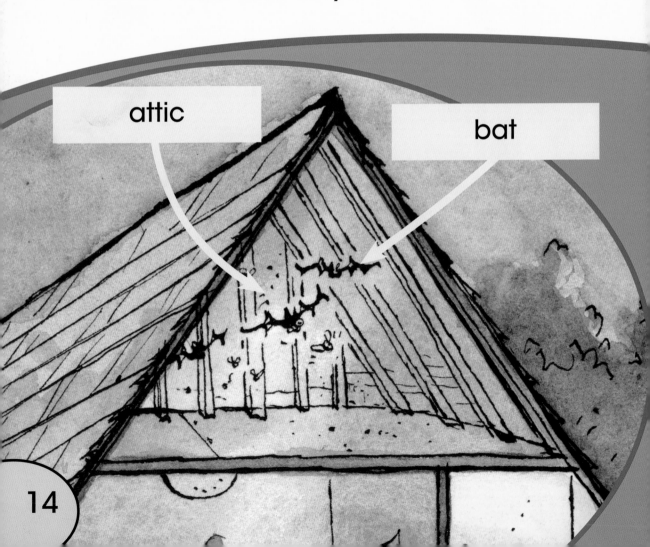

attic

bat

## FUN FACT

Most bats do not use their eyes to see at night. Instead they use their ears to hear sounds that bounce off objects around them.

# Bat Snacks

Many bats eat insects. Some bats eat wasps and beetles. Some bats eat moths and small bugs called **gnats**. They can eat hundreds or even thousands of insects a night.

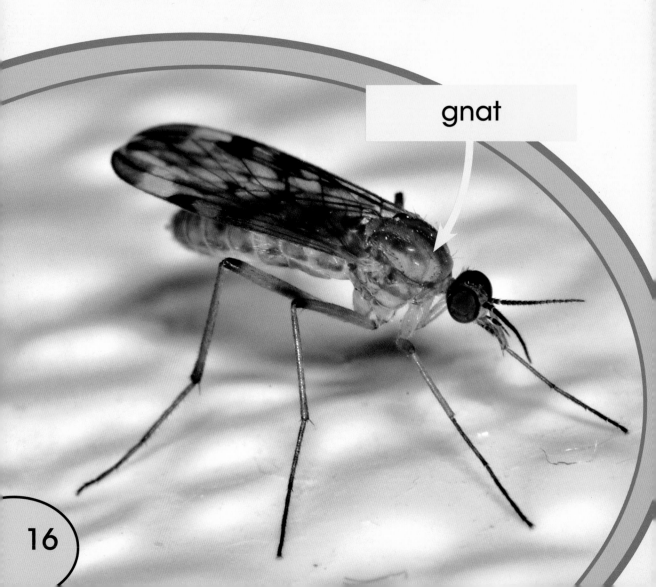

gnat

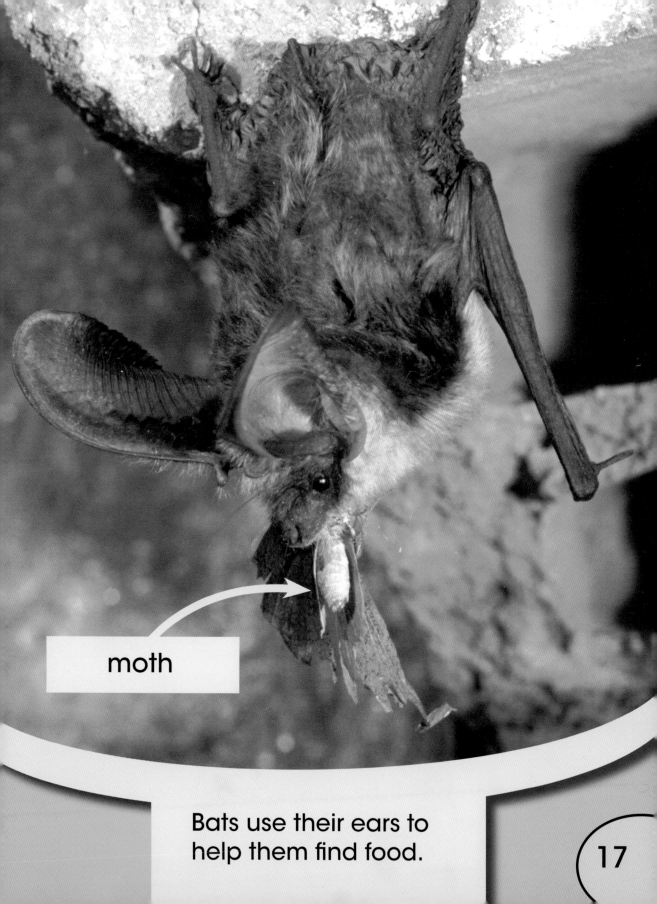

moth

Bats use their ears to
help them find food.

thumb

fingers

## FUN FACT

Bats have very long fingers compared to the size of their bodies. If we had fingers like a bat, they would be as long as our legs!

Bats are **nocturnal**. This means they sleep during the day and fly around at night. When you are in bed, stay still and listen. You may hear bats flying around your house.

# Scratch, Scratch!

Rats are **mammals**. They have four legs, a tail, and fur. Rats could be living in the walls or ceiling. They could be living under the floor.

Do you hear scratching at night? It might be rats.

Rats often eat at night. They like to eat nuts and fruit. They like to eat meat and fish. When you wake up, look in your kitchen. You might find rat droppings, or poo, in your food.

rat poo

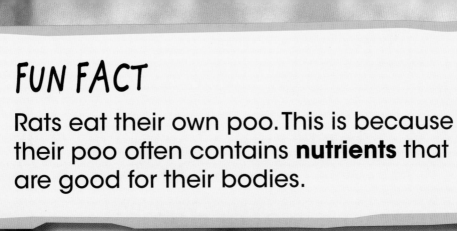

A garbage can is a great place for a rat to find a snack!

23

# Mold

Mold is a small living thing. Mold likes to live in warm places. Mold can only live where it is wet or **damp**.

mold

mold

**FUN FACT**

Mold needs water to stay alive. So if you get rid of the moisture, you get rid of the mold!

mold

Mold can live in many places. It can live on walls and floors. It can live on wallpaper and carpet. It can live on tiles and pipes. Mold can make you sick.

mold

# Keeping It Clean and Dry

Your walls and floors hold up your house. When you see holes, repair them. When you see food crumbs, clean them up. This will help you keep creatures and mold away.

# Fun Facts

Termites don't like light. They can even die from being in direct sunlight.

One of the smallest types of bat is the bumblebee bat. It is about as long as a paperclip.

A single bat can eat up to 600 mosquitoes in just 60 minutes.

Baby bats are called pups, just like dogs.

Like us, rats have belly buttons.

Unlike us, rats can't **vomit**.

# Glossary

**attic** room, or space, under the roof of a house

**colony** group of termites or other insects that are living in one place

**damp** wet or moist

**gnat** type of small insect

**mammal** type of warm-blooded animal that gets milk from its mother when it is a baby. It also has fur or hair on its body.

**nocturnal** describes animals that sleep during the daytime and come out at night

**nutrients** things that animals and plants need to stay healthy. Food contains nutrients.

**roost** place where a bat sleeps

**vomit** another word for puke, or to be sick

**worker termite** type of termite that brings food to the rest of the colony

# Find Out More

## Books

Wilson, Natashya. *Bats.* New York: Rosen, 2004.

Murray, Peter. *Insects.* Mankato, MN: Child's World, 2005.

Rustad, Martha. *Termites.* Minneapolis: Bellwether Media, 2008.

Wade, Mary Dodson. *Tiny Life on the Ground.* Danbury, CT: Children's Press, 2005.

## Websites

**http://www.pestworldforkids.org/rats.html**
This Website tells you about rats in general and describes two types of rats.

**http://www.kids-science-experiments.com/growingmold.html**
This Website contains a science experiment on how to grow mold.

**Find out**

What do rats make their nests out of?

# Index